Christmas Favorites

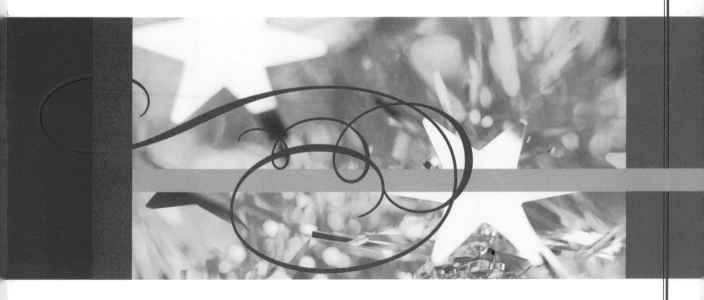

Christmas
Favorites

*your favorite holiday music
in words, pictures and audio*

sourcebooks
mediaFusion

An Imprint of Sourcebooks Inc.®
Naperville, Illinois

Musical recordings under license from Naxos of America Inc., www.naxos.com. (P)
2001 HNH International Ltd. All rights reserved. Unlawful duplication, broadcast or
performance of this disc is prohibited by applicable law. Scores and lyrics for "Deck the
Hall," "Good King Wenceslas," "The Holly and the Ivy," "Lo, How a Rose E'er Bloom-
ing," "The First Nowell," "O Christmas Tree," "Joy to the World," "For Unto Us a
Child is Born" and "Hallelujah Chorus" from Handel's *Messiah*, "Hark the Herald
Angels Sing," "Silent Night," "What Child is This," "Away in a Manger," "Jingle Bells,"
"Sleigh Ride" by L. Anderson and P. Mitchell, and "Santa Claus is Coming to Town" ©
Warner Brothers Publications. Score and lyrics for "Rudolph the Red Nosed Reindeer"
by J. Marks © St. Nicholas Music Inc.

Published by Sourcebooks, Inc.
P.O. Box 4410, Naperville, Illinois 60567-4410
(630) 961-3900
FAX: (630) 961-2168
www.sourcebooks.com

ISBN 1-4022-0325-X
Printed and bound in the United States of America
VHG 10 9 8 7 6 5 4 3 2 1

dedicated to all those who love the wonderful music of Christmas

Contents

Foreword

What would Christmas be without music? Christmas carols express the central message of the Christmas story and reinforce the priceless themes of generosity of spirit, peace on earth, and joy in salvation. Secular favorites echo the fun and delight of the holiday season. Whether heard in family gatherings around the Christmas tree or caroling door-to-door, in shopping malls or church services, Christmas music is a uniting force that can wonderfully engage the human soul. Since the early centuries of Christianity, when primitive chants and the singing of Latin hymns were a primary aspect of religious celebration, Christmas music—in one form or another—has been a perennial joy shared by celebrants around the world.

The word "carol" may have been derived from a number of sources, including the Greek word *charos,* the Anglo-Saxon word *kyrriole,* medieval dances called *carolles* or *karolles,* or the French word *carole.* Originally the word carol referred to a round dance. In later years it would be defined as a joyful religious song and today most people think of carols as strictly Christmas songs. It is estimated that at least four to five thousand carols exist, most of them in the realm of the obscure.

The development of carols coincided with that of folk songs and polyphonic music, although medieval carol settings were derived from an even simpler art form. Carols essentially began as unpretentious songs of the common people—before clerics and trained musicians claimed them. They had simple lyrics that were easily understood, and they reflected the religious (as well as secular) impulses of the people. It is likely minstrels and troubadours, who composed and sang poems mostly of a secular nature, sang carols as they traveled from town to hamlet during the Christmas season.

However, there is very little record of folk or non-liturgical music in the Western world until the late Middle Ages, save for precious few examples of notated secular music. There are many documents that provide evidence for (or against) the practice of music in the church, which of itself constitutes a rich history. To fully appreciate the origins of Christmas music, it is necessary to understand the link between Western music and Christian liturgy.

The celebration of Christmas was a lot less elaborate in the first three centuries of Christianity, as early believers suffered serious religious persecution and martyrdom at the hands of Roman emperors. Early Christian communities continued some musical practices of the Jewish synagogue. The liturgical organization of the Mass was partly based on the Jewish order of services, and the nature of church chant was a melting pot of Jewish, Syrian, and Greek musical systems. The cantor would sing psalm verses and the congregation a simple refrain.

During the early centuries of developing Christianity, the birth of Christ was considered the commemoration of a historical event as opposed to a mystery feast of the church, such as Easter. Very little sacred Christmas music was composed or known to exist. With the advancement of Latin hymns by St. Ambrose of Milan and St. Hiliary of Poitiers, as well as the fifth century papal declaration of December 25 as the liturgical celebration of the Mystery of the Incarnation and thus a major feast day, Christmas began to have higher profile.

The elevation of the importance of Christmas was reflected in church chant, which was quite diverse until Pope Gregory decreed that the immense store of liturgical chant should be unified. Because of his efforts, chant thereafter would be named after him, although it was not until the ninth century that it would be universally accepted as the official music of the church. Gregorian chant, though it was not permitted to be accompanied by musical instruments, had become more sophisticated by the twelfth century as a result of cumulative developments in musical notation, particularly the invention of the musical staff by Guido d'Arezzo, a Dominican monk. It was also a period when Church officials, in their struggles to ward off the influence of secularism and pagan customs, were loathe to permit the singing of carols inside of church walls because many of them came from pagan sources or used to be sung to profane words.

In the meantime, the mystery plays of the fourteenth and fifteenth century—staged reenactments of biblical scenes—helped to popularize the singing of carols. One of the oldest of folk customs, carols and their conveyance of good tidings emerged during the late Middle Ages and early stages of the Renaissance. During this era, when most people were illiterate and few understood Latin—the universal language of the European continent and the Christian Church—the popularity of carols blossomed in the countryside. St. Francis of Assisi, the much-honored saint, was said to have encouraged the singing of carols when he was the first to erect a crèche in an outdoor setting where ordinary people could worship and celebrate Christmas Midnight Mass.

For the church, changes were on the horizon. By the fourteenth century it was losing its influence on the everyday affairs of its people due to various abuses of the clergy. In the sphere of music, this disengagement contributed to the composition of more secular music, the inspiration for which was found in the non-liturgical world, and the marked increase in vernacular carols. Gregorian chant, the preferred music of the Christian Church, began to be eclipsed by a new music, or *Ars Nova*.

Gregorian chant, or plainchant, was monophonic music, and no matter how many voices participated, they all sang the same note unsupported by harmony. In the area of rhythm, a major achievement of the *Ars Nova*, polyphonic compositions allowed for three, four, five, or even six different voices to sing in a complex weave of individual melodies. Despite initial resistance, these advanced musical practices began to find acceptance in some ecclesiastical circles, and after the Reformation they were readily adopted by Martin Luther.

Luther sought reforms in music, just as he sought change in theology and ethics. He loved carols and polyphony and he wanted music that would move people by fusing faith and song. The Reformation leader encouraged greater participation by the congregation in singing, and he simplified the music from choir plainsong to easy harmony. The more conservative Roman Church, however, still favored all-male choirs to sing the church repertory, and it would be centuries before non-Latin Christmas carols or hymns were included in church hymnals.

The Lutheran choral style, when enjoined with soaring instrumental music in the seventeenth and eighteenth century, led to the exalted sacred works of Johann Sebastian Bach—notably his cantatas and oratorios—and George Frederic Handel—especially his oratorio, *Messiah*. The aftereffects of the Reformation also extended the range of choral music beyond the liturgy, and the informal group singing of songs was highly encouraged, leading to a greater familiarity with Christmas hymns.

The new choral methods of singing hymns and carols were emulated by English and American churches after the decline of Puritanism. The Puritans had banned music in church as well as the celebration of Christmas. They even went so far as to declare Christmas a working day. Because of the Puritan outreach, the growth of carols in the English-speaking world was stunted for two hundred years; but people from the countryside kept carols alive by singing them in private.

With the waning of the Puritan influence and the frequent nineteenth- and twentieth-century publication of carol books, the tradition of singing carols both inside and outside of churches became common practice. The tradition of caroling was perpetuated in English towns by city employees or watchmen, known as waits, who sang carols on their night rounds or for town-sponsored holiday festivities. With the invention of less expensive printing processes by the early nineteenth century, traditional carol books were more readily available and the public soon snapped them up for carol rounds or private enjoyment. It was also during the nineteenth century that caroling door-to-door became fashionable.

Although Christmas is primarily a religious holiday, the addition of tuneful secular songs over the centuries has brought a pleasant spice to the Christmas-music mix. The contributions come from many diverse sources: compositions of mid-twentieth century American songwriters, melodic *alleluias* sung by their predecessors of several millennia ago, canting of the ancient synagogue, and the contributions of so many anonymous carol composers, all help to make the music of the Christmas season both delightful and meaningful.

Today, as the holidays approach, from churches and concert halls comes the sound of sacred hymns, classical works, and favorite carols. From radio stations and shopping malls come recordings of holiday classics. Christmas music fans revel in the favorite songs of their youth as "Jingle Bells" and "Rudolph the Red-Nosed Reindeer" dance on their lips, just as "Silent Night" and "Away in a Manger" move their souls. Whatever your age, your holiday season will be brighter and merrier with the sound of *Christmas Favorites*.

Ronald M. Clancy
Christmas Music Historian
Author of *Christmas Classics*

Christmas
Favorites

your favorite holiday music in words, pictures and audio

Deck the Halls with Boughs of Holly

Other Title: Deck the Halls
Words & Music:
Anonymous, sixteenth-
century Welsh folk song

Very little is known about the origins of this familiar and popular Welsh carol. The melody can be found in a 1784 song collection titled *Musical and Poetical Relicks of the Welsh Bards*, but it is associated with another Welsh carol known as "Nos Galan" (meaning "New Year's Eve"). Wolfgang Amadeus Mozart (1756–1791), the great Austrian composer, used the melody for one of his compositions, a duet for violin and piano.

The cheerful lyrics, whose first known printing was in the 1881 New York publication *The Franklin Square Song Collection*, are sometimes thought to have originated in America, perhaps because Washington Irving, a nineteenth-century author and devotee of English traditions and customs, was influential in encouraging carol composing and singing in America. By his time, the constraining Puritan influence on Christmas customs had been loosened both in England and the United States and the Christmas celebration was being reinvented.

One of our merriest and most energetic Christmas carols, "Deck the Halls with Boughs of Holly," is sung in the style of madrigals, which were quite popular in the sixteenth century and whose refrains, with nonsense words such as "fa la la la la la la la la," followed each line of verse.

Deck the halls with boughs of holly,
fa la la la la la la la la.
'Tis the season to be jolly,
fa la la la la la la la la.
Don we now our gay apparel,
fa la la la la la la la la.
Troll the ancient Yuletide carol,
fa la la la la la la la la.

See the blazing Yule before us,
fa la la la la la la la la.
Strike the harp and join the chorus,
fa la la la la la la la la.
Follow me in merry measure,
fa la la la la la la la la.
While I tell of Yuletide treasure,
fa la la la la la la la la.

Fast away the old year passes,
fa la la la la la la la la.
Hail the new, ye lads and lasses,
fa la la la la la la la la.
Sing we joyous all together,
fa la la la la la la la la.
Heedless of the wind and weather,
fa la la la la la la la la!

DECK THE HALLS

OLD WELSH AIR

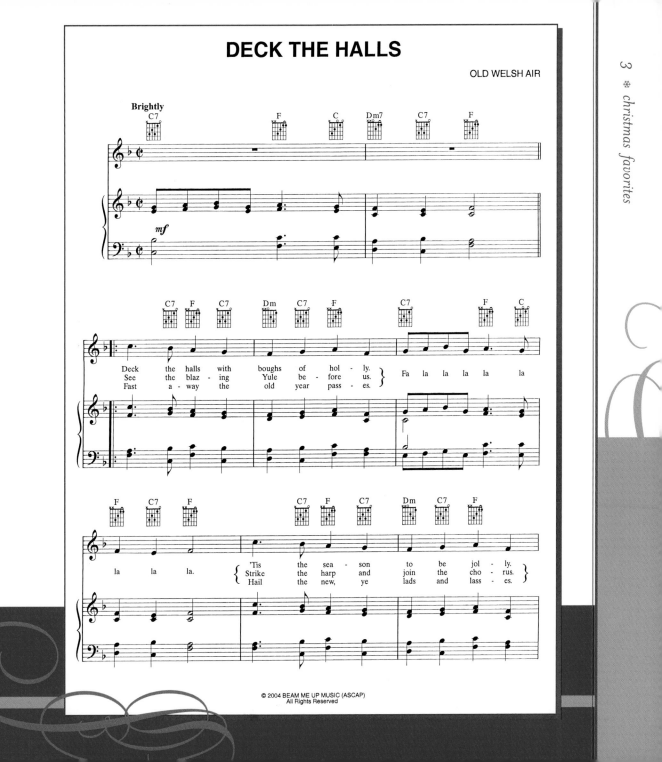

Jingle Bells

*Other Title: One Horse
Open Sleigh
Words & Music: James S.
Pierpont (1822–1893),
American author*

Probably the best-known American secular Christmas song, "Jingle Bells" was written in 1857 (or perhaps earlier) by James S. Pierpont. It was first performed at a Thanksgiving program at his Boston church, where he also taught Sunday school. Pierpont was the son of John Pierpont (1785–1866), an abolitionist poet and minister, and the uncle of John Pierpont Morgan (1837–1913), the great American financier. Surprisingly, during the Civil War, James wrote several war songs popular with the Confederacy. Initially titled "One Horse Open Sleigh," the song was quickly learned by Pierpont's Sunday school children because his lyrics were so clear and simple.

There is an unsubstantiated anecdote claiming the title was changed to "Jingle Bells" because one of the composer's friends commented that the piece was a delightful jingle, but the many repetitions of the phrase made such a change entirely natural, if not predictable. Judging by the number of recording artists who have released this jaunty tune, "Jingle Bells" holds a very special place in the American holiday song repertoire and in the hearts of Christmas lovers.

REFRAIN:
Jingle bells, jingle bells,
jingle all the way;
Oh, what fun it is to ride
in a one-horse open sleigh.
Jingle bells, jingle bells,
jingle all the way;
Oh, what fun it is to ride
in a one-horse open sleigh!

Dashing through the snow
in a one-horse open sleigh;
O'er the fields we go,
laughing all the way.
Bells on bobtail ring,
making spirits bright;
What fun it is to ride and sing
a sleighing song tonight.
REFRAIN

A day or two ago
I thought I'd take a ride,
and soon Miss Fannie Bright
was seated by my side.
The horse was lean and lank,
misfortune seem'd his lot.
He got into a drifted bank,
and then we got upsot!

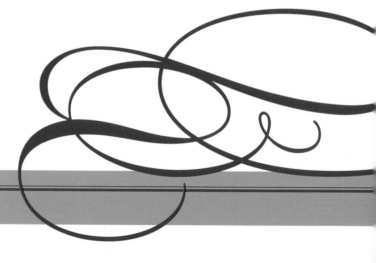

JINGLE BELLS

Words and Music by
JAMES PIERPONT

Good King Wenceslas

Words: John Mason Neale
(1818–1866),
English minister
Music: Anonymous,
thirteenth-century
northern European

The Rev. John Mason Neale, who published the English lyrics to "Good King Wenceslas" in *Carols for Christmas-tide* (1854), was looking for a good role model for children. The generous Wenceslas fit the description nicely. Neale's fanciful lyrics, which drew scorn from his critics, were based on the story of the nobleman Wenceslas (c.907–929), Duke of Bohemia, a kind and good man who was raised by his devoted grandmother. Wenceslas became king, and during his brief reign he converted his country to Christianity and provided his people with a period of great peace and serenity. It was his decree that Christmas should be celebrated in every cottage and church throughout the land.

Wenceslas was known to be a just and merciful king with considerable compassion for the poor and sick. Unfortunately for his people, Wenceslas was murdered in 929 by a younger brother who conspired against him with other family members and the pagan nobility.

The music for "Good King Wenceslas" comes from an anonymous thirteenth-century Swedish spring carol titled "Tempest Adest Floridum," part of the 1582 carol book publication *Piae Cantiones*. "Good King Wenceslas," despite its confounding lyrics, has become a Christmas favorite for children and adults alike.

*Good King Wenceslas look'd out
on the feast of Stephen,
when the snow lay round about,
deep and crisp and even.
Brightly shone the moon that night,
though the frost was cruel,
when a poor man came in sight,
gath'ring winter fuel.*

*"Hither, page, and stand by me,
if thou know'st it, telling,
yonder peasant, who is he?
Where and what his dwelling?
"Sire, he lives a good league hence,
underneath the mountain;
Right against the forest fence,
by Saint Agnes' fountain."*

*"Bring me flesh and bring me wine,
bring me pine logs hither.
Thou and I will see him dine,
when we bear him thither."*

*Page and monarch forth they went,
forth they went together,
through the rude wind's wild lament
and the bitter weather.*

*"Sire, the night is darker now,
and the wind blows stronger.
Fails my heart, I know not how,
I can go no longer."
"Mark my footsteps, my good page,
tread thou in them boldly.
Thou shalt find the winter's rage
freeze thy blood less coldly."*

*In his master's steps he trod,
where the snow lay dinted.
Heat was in the very sod
which the saint had printed.
Therefore, Christian men, be sure,
wealth or rank possessing;
Ye who now will bless the poor
shall yourselves find blessing.*

GOOD KING WENCESLAS

TRADITIONAL

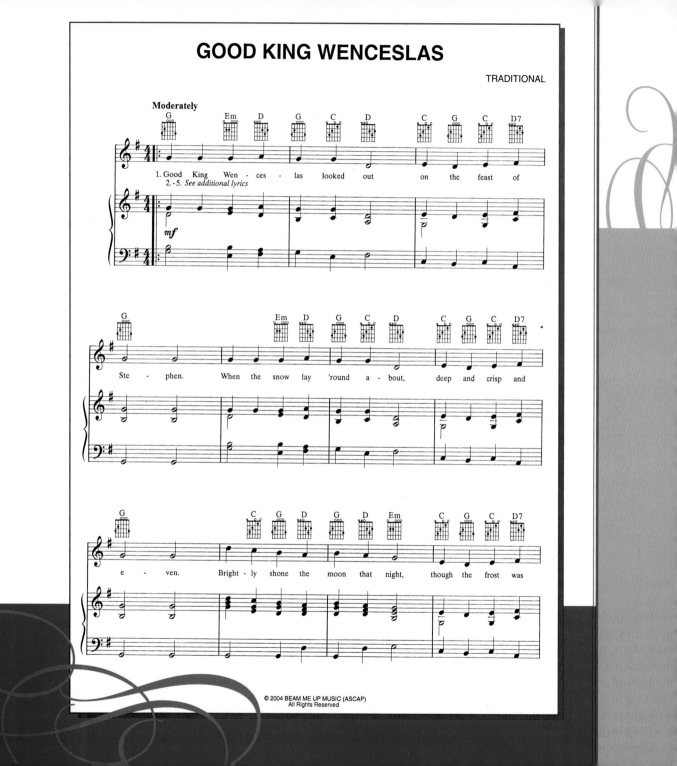

G   Em   D7   Em   D   G   C   G   D7

cru - el,   when   a   poor   man   came   in   sight,   gath - 'ring   win - ter

Em   C   G   D7   G

1.-4.   5.

fu - el.   ing,

2. "Hither, page, and stand by me,
   If thou know'st it, telling.
   Yonder peasant, who is he?
   Where and what his dwelling?"
   "Sire, he lives a good league hence,
   Underneath the mountain:
   Right against the forest fence,
   By Saint Agnes' fountain."

3. "Bring me flesh and bring me wine,
   Bring me pine logs hither.
   Thou and I will see him dine,
   When we bear him thither."
   Page and monrch forth they went,
   Forth they went together,
   Through the rude wind's wild lament
   And the bitter weather.

4. "Sire, the night is darker now,
   And the wind blows stronger.
   Fails my heart, I know not how,
   I can go no longer."
   "Mark my footsteps, my good page,
   Tread thou in them boldly.
   Thou shalt find the winter's rage
   Freeze thy blood less coldly."

5. In his master's steps he trod,
   Where the snow lay dinted.
   Heat was in the very sod
   Which the Saint had printed.
   Therefore, Christian men, be sure,
   Wealth or rank posessing;
   Ye who now will bless the poor
   Shall yourselves find blessing.

Messiah

Chorus:
For Unto Us a Child Is Born

Words: Biblical texts
selected by Charles Jennens
(1700–1773), English
poet and librettist
Music: George Frederic
Handel (1685–1759),
German-born English composer

Born in Halle, Germany, George Frederic Handel emigrated to England in 1710 to further enhance his career in music and opera. Thirty-one years later, between August 22 and September 14, 1741, the great composer wrote *Messiah*, an oratorio based upon both Old and New Testament texts, artfully strung together by Charles Jennens.

Messiah told the story of the life of Jesus Christ, from birth to resurrection, in an extremely compressed form.

Handel responded to Jennens's work with a great deal of enthusiasm. After beginning the arduous task of composition in London, Handel—who brought the oratorio style of music to an unprecedented level of development—worked feverishly to complete this masterpiece, hardly stopping for rest. During the writing of the "Hallelujah Chorus," he grew so ecstatic that he called in his manservant and declared to him in a tearfully joyous manner, "I did think I did see all heaven before me, and the great God Himself."

Since the work was intended for Easter festivities, the first performance of it took place on April 13, 1742, in Dublin, Ireland, where both the composer and the initial performance of *Messiah* were very warmly received. When Handel's *Messiah* went to the London stage, however, it took many performances before the oratorio gained universal popularity. Today *Messiah* is widely acclaimed and regarded by some musicologists as one of the Western world's finest compositions.

The last performance of *Messiah* conducted by Handel himself occurred on April 16, 1759 at the Foundling Hospital in London. Eight days later Handel died. Today Handel's remains rest at Westminster Abbey, one of the most hallowed shrines in London.

Over the years Handel's masterpiece has increasingly been performed during the Christmas season, even though the major emphasis of the work is the eventful Passion of Christ.

For Unto Us a Child Is Born

One of the more familiar choruses of the *Messiah*, "For Unto Us a Child Is Born" exclaims that the newborn Child shall hold many majestic titles, as promised by the prophetic words of Isaiah 9:6 that serve as the text for the lyrics.

For unto us a Child is born,
unto us a Son is given.
And the government shall be upon his shoulder.
And His name shall be called:
Wonderful Counsellor,
the Mighty God,
the Everlasting Father,
the Prince of Peace.

FOR UNTO US A CHILD IS BORN
(from "The Messiah")

Words and Music by
GEORGE FREDERICk HANDEL

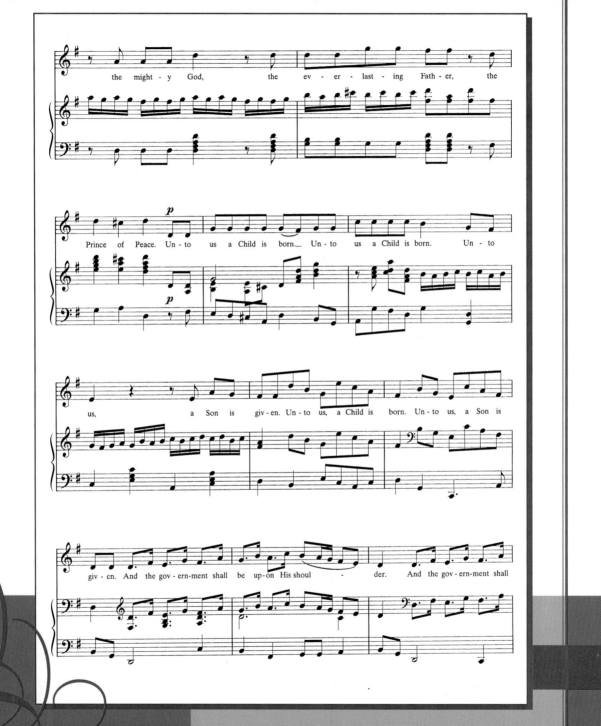

The Holly and the Ivy

*Words & Music:
Anonymous, late
seventeenth or early
eighteenth century
English folk song*

Although the standard text and the tune of this traditional English carol were published in the 1911 volume *English Folk-Carols*, the first strains of "The Holly and the Ivy" may have come from the days of Geoffrey Chaucer (1340–1400), originating from the Somerset and Gloucestershire vicinity.

For centuries, holly and ivy were viewed as important symbols, and they came to be associated particularly with the Christmas season. In songs of Yuletide, the holly and ivy plants represented the different genders—the holly was masculine, and the ivy was feminine. Often these symbols were used in comical verse. During the Middle Ages, it was common for homes and churches to be decorated with holly because village folks believed it kept witches and tax collectors away. Ivy was of pagan heritage in keeping with wreaths worn by Bacchus, the Roman wine god. It was common to dance around evergreen plants that did not die in winter, a practice stemming from the pagan celebration of the winter solstice.

Eventually the holly and the ivy took on much more religious associations. Wreaths made from holly represented Jesus Christ's crown of thorns and its red berries signified drops of red blood.

There is some argument that the carol originated in France, but it most certainly comes from England. It is interesting to note that, despite the title, the ivy is mentioned only once, in the first line of the song.

The holly and the ivy,
when they are both full grown,
of all the trees that are in the wood,
the holly bears the crown.

REFRAIN:
The rising of the sun
and the running of the deer,
the playing of the merry organ,
sweet singing in the choir.

The holly bears a blossom
as white as lily flow'r;
And Mary bore sweet Jesus Christ
to be our sweet Savior.
REFRAIN

The holly bears a berry
as red as any blood,
and Mary bore sweet Jesus Christ
to do poor sinners good.
REFRAIN

The holly bears a prickle
as sharp as any thorn;
And Mary bore sweet Jesus Christ
on Christmas Day in the morn.
REFRAIN

The holly bears a bark
as bitter as any gall;
And Mary bore sweet Jesus Christ
for to redeem us all.
REFRAIN

THE HOLLY AND THE IVY

Traditional English

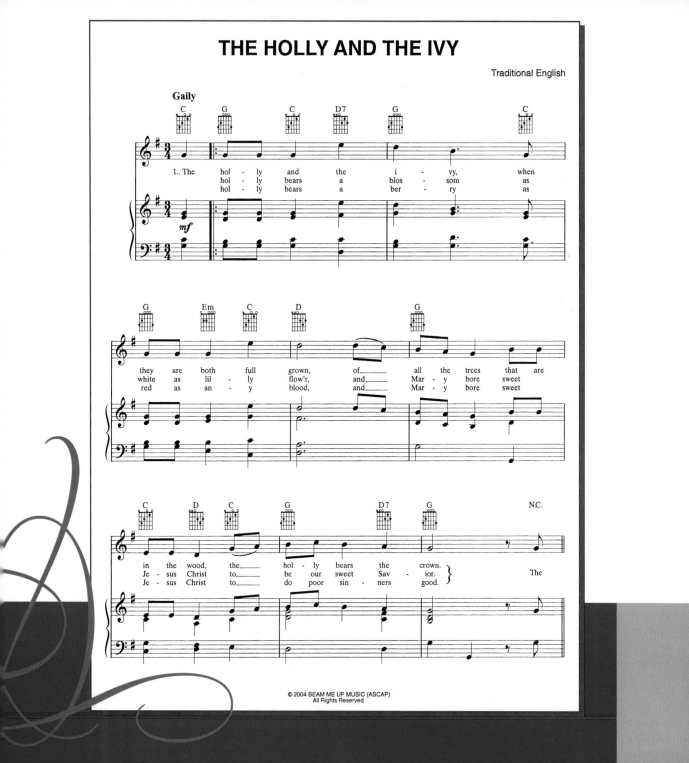

Santa Claus Is Comin' to Town

Words: Haven Gillespie (1888–1975), American songwriter
Music: John Frederick Coots (1897–1985), American composer

The modern image of a jolly Santa Claus was made popular by Thomas Nast (1840–1902), a noted German-born American illustrator and political cartoonist, about fifty years after Clement Clark Moore's poem "A Visit from St. Nicholas" (also known as "'Twas the Night Before Christmas") was first published. Nast, known also for creating the political symbols of an elephant for the Republican Party and a donkey for the Democratic Party, was rather fond of Santa Claus and stories about him. He went on to create a number of Santa Claus illustrations for the *Harper's Weekly*, a periodical with which he enjoyed a long association, first on a free-lance basis and then as a regular from 1862, the height of the Civil War, until 1888. It is probable that Nast's Santa Claus served as the model for the familiar rosy-cheek Santa of the twentieth century.

Although "Santa Claus Is Comin' to Town" was composed in 1932 by Haven Gillespie and John Frederick Coots, the song did not receive immediate attention. Two years later at Thanksgiving time, Ida Cantor persuaded her husband, Eddie Cantor (1892–1964), to give the song a chance on his popular national radio program. The song became an immediate success. George Hall and his Orchestra, with vocalist Sonny Schuyler, released it as a recording and it rose to the number-twelve spot on pop music charts during the 1934 Christmas season. In 1947, Bing Crosby and the Andrews Sisters also enjoyed a successful recording of the song. Ranked in the *Top 100 Most-Recorded Songs* in the history of modern music, "Santa Claus Is Comin' to Town" is one of the season's more memorable tunes and continues to bring listening pleasure to children and parents alike.

You better watch out, you better not cry,
Better not pout, I'm telling you why:
Santa Claus is comin' to town.
He's making a list and checking it twice;
Gonna find out who's naughty and nice.
Santa Claus is comin' to town.

He sees you when you're sleepin'.
He knows when you're awake.
He knows if you've been bad or good,
so be good for goodness sake.
Oh, you better watch out, you better not cry,
Better not pout, I'm telling you why:
Santa Claus is comin' to town.

SANTA CLAUS IS COMIN' TO TOWN

Moderately

Words and Music by
J.FRED COOTS and HAVEN GILLESPIE

You bet-ter watch out, you bet-ter not cry, bet-ter not pout, I'm tell-ing you why:

San - ta Claus is com - in' to town. He's

mak-ing a list and check-ing it twice. Gon-na find out who's naught-y and nice:

San - ta Claus is com - in' to town._____ He

Rudolph the Red-Nosed Reindeer

Words & Music:
Johnny Marks
(1909–1985),
American songwriter

Johnny Marks had a great knack for composing Christmas holiday songs; "Rudolph the Red-Nosed Reindeer" was the first of several gems he produced (e.g. "Most Wonderful Time of the Year," "Rockin' Around the Christmas Tree" and "Holly Jolly Christmas"). The story of the intrepid little reindeer—who turns what seems to be a liability into an asset and saves the day on Christmas—became an immediate big seller in 1949 when it was first recorded by Gene Autry (1907–1998) of motion picture and singing cowboy fame.

However, it was Johnny Marks's brother-in-law, Robert May, who invented the familiar character of Rudolph. Rudolph had been born ten years earlier, as part of a 1939

Christmas promotional campaign for May's employer, Montgomery Ward, the national department store chain. Reindeer have been associated with the modern myth of Santa Claus since Clement Moore developed it in his classic poem "'Twas the Night Before Christmas." May used Moore's reindeer cast of characters and created a colorful story that became an instant sensation. Children who came to visit Santa Claus at Montgomery Ward stores were given a free copy of the story booklet, illustrated by Denver Gillen, and for several years millions more of this eagerly sought item were dispensed in similar fashion.

When Johnny Marks wrote the first draft of "Rudolph the Red-Nosed Reindeer," he thought it was the worst song he had ever composed. About a year later, while walking in Greenwich Village in New York, he finally solved a musical obstacle he had had with the initial draft. Marks then sent a demo of his new song to Gene Autry, who initially ruled it out, saying he felt that it didn't fit his cowboy image. But Autry's wife, Ina Mae, was enthusiastic about the song, and asked her husband to record it as a favor to her. "Put it on the B side," she said, "and put whatever you want on the A side."

Autry took his wife's advice, and, as luck would have it, the song became the biggest hit of his career and in the history of Columbia Records (recordings of the song by more than five hundred different performers have sold more than 170 million copies). Although not the only novelty carol to appear in the post-World War II period, Rudolph became the prototype for many popular Christmas novelty songs to follow.

You know Dasher and Dancer and Prancer and Vixen,
Comet and Cupid and Donner and Blitzen,
but do you recall
the most famous reindeer of all?

Rudolph the red-nosed Reindeer
had a very shiny nose,
and if you ever saw it,
you would even say it glows.

All of the other reindeer
used to laugh and call him names;
They never let poor Rudolph
join in any reindeer games.

Then one foggy Christmas Eve
Santa came to say,
"Rudolph with your nose so bright,
won't you guide my sleigh tonight?"

Then how the reindeer loved him,
as they shouted out with glee,
"Rudolph the red-nosed Reindeer,
you'll go down in history."

RUDOLPH THE RED-NOSED REINDEER

Words and Music by
JOHNNY MARKS

Away in a Manger

Words: Anonymous,
eighteenth- or
nineteenth-century
American folk song
Music: James Ramsey
Murray (1841–1905),
American composer

A well-known carol hymn of somewhat obscure origins, "Away in a Manger" was apparently composed in the late nineteenth century by a member of the German Lutheran colony in Pennsylvania. For years, the hymn was thought to have been composed by Martin Luther, the great German religious reformer, and it was often referred to as "Luther's Cradle Hymn." However, by the 1940s it was proven conclusively that the music was actually composed by James Ramsey Murray, who had himself perpetrated the myth of "Luther's Cradle Hymn." (Murray, perhaps heady from the Christmas experience, allowed his fanciful imagination to get the better of him.) He published his lullaby in an 1887 Cincinnati collection called *Dainty Songs for Lads and Lasses*. Since then, at least forty-one known tunes have been associated with the carol, including those of Jonathan E. Spilman (1812–1896) and William J. Kirkpatrick (1838–1921), whose familiar settings are more likely to be heard in England.

The words for the first two stanzas of "Away in a Manger" first appeared several years earlier (1885) in the *Little Children's Book for Schools and Families*, a publication of the Evangelical Lutheran Church in North America. These words may have come from an 1883 poem commemorating the four hundredth anniversary of the birth of Martin Luther. Although many modern hymnals attribute the lyrics of the third stanza to John T. McFarland (1851–1913), a member of the American Lutheran Board of Sunday Schools, it is believed he merely made reference to it. This third stanza, which first appeared in an 1892 Louisville, Kentucky, Lutheran Church collection titled *Gabriel's Vineyard Songs*, is probably the contribution of another anonymous author. A lyrical addition, it strengthens the inherent tenderness of the renowned American carol hymn.

Away in a manger, no crib for His bed,
the little Lord Jesus lay down His sweet head.
The stars in the heavens looked down where He lay;
The little Lord Jesus asleep in the hay.

The cattle are lowing, the poor baby wakes,
but little Lord Jesus no crying He makes.
I love Thee, Lord Jesus, look down from the sky,
and stay by my cradle to watch lullaby.

Be near me, Lord Jesus, I ask Thee to stay
close by me forever and love me I pray.
Bless all the dear children in Thy tender care,
and take us to heaven to live with Thee there.

AWAY IN A MANGER

Words and Music by
J.E. SPILLMAN
and MARTIN LUTHER

Joy to the World

*Words: Isaac Watts
(1674–1748), English
poet and clergyman
Music: Lowell Mason
(1792–1872),
American composer*

Another carol first written as a poem, "Joy to the World" was the creation of the great hymn composer, Isaac Watts. The words were first published in 1719, in *Psalms of David Imitated in the Language of the New Testament.* Watts may have found inspiration for his poem from Psalm 98:4–9 of the Old Testament, particularly the verse lines, "Make a joyful noise unto the Lord, all the earth."

One of the first tunes that seems to have been associated with the text was "Antioch" by George Frederic Handel (1685–1759), the famous Baroque composer, as suggested in the 1833 publication *T. Hawkes Collection of Tunes.* However, a number of other composers have also been connected with this tune, bringing some measure of doubt that Handel arranged it.

Lowell Mason, the leading Presbyterian hymn-composer in the United States, first united his magnificent tune with Watts's text in 1836. The two have since been inseparable. A popular carol that has become a staple among Christmas offerings, "Joy to the World" bursts forth in triumphant exultation about the good news of Christ's birth.

Joy to the world! The Lord is come;
Let earth receive her King.
Let ev'ry heart prepare Him room,
and heav'n and nature sing,
and heav'n and nature sing,
and heav'n, and heav'n and nature sing.

Joy to the earth! The Savior reigns;
Let men their songs employ.
While fields and floods, rocks, hills and plains
repeat the sounding joy,
repeat the sounding joy,
repeat, repeat the sounding joy.

He rules the world with truth and grace,
and makes the nations prove
the glories of His righteousness
and wonders of His love,
and wonders of His love,
and wonders, wonders of His love.

JOY TO THE WORLD

Words by
ISAAC WATTS

Music by
GEORGE F. HANDEL

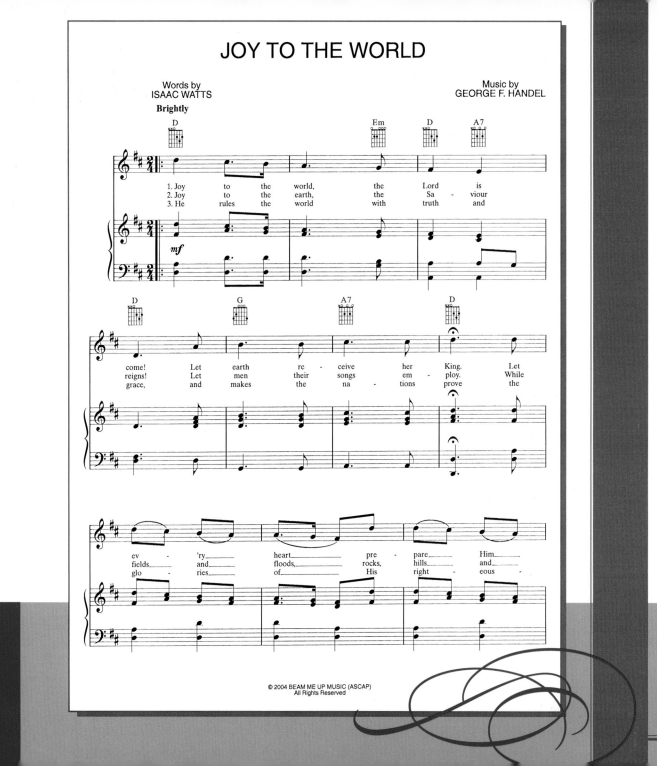

Lo, How a Rose E'er Blooming

German Title: Es ist ein' Ros' entsprungen
Words & Music: Anonymous, fifteenth-century German folk song

The original version of the exquisite "Lo, How a Rose E'er Blooming" may have come from the German Rhineland with no less than twenty-two stanzas. Later reduced to a mere sixteen-stanza piece, the carol is now normally sung in one, two, or three stanzas. The carol has had several English translations, including the first two stanzas here by noted American music scholar, Theodore Baker (1851–1934). There are a number of other titles and interesting arrangements, including an 1896 chorale prelude by Johannes Brahms (1833–1897).

The music was first published in a 1599 Catholic hymnal from Cologne and the lyrics appeared in another publication the same year. Michael Praetorius (1571–1621), one of the most distinguished composers of his time and the greatest master of Protestant church music, harmonized the folk tune and published his version in 1609. Praetorius, who was highly influenced by Italian baroque music, used the Lutheran chorale texts as the basis for many of his church compositions. "Lo, How a Rose E'er Blooming," a favorite of *a cappella* choirs during the Christmas season, is an example of this Praetorius technique. The inspiration for the carol is found in Isaiah 11:1: "And there shall come forth a rod out of the stem of Jesse, and a Branch shall grow out of his roots."

Lo, how a rose e'er blooming
from tender stem hath sprung.
Of Jesse's lineage coming,
as men of old have sung.
It came a floweret bright
amid the cold of winter,
when half spent was the night.

Isaiah 'twas foretold it,
the rose I have in mind.
With Mary we behold it,
the virgin Mother kind.
To show God's love aright,
she bore to me a Savior
when half spent was the night.

This Flow'r, whose fragrance tender
with sweetness fills the air,
dispels with glorious splendor
the darkness ev'rywhere.
True man, yet very God;
from sin and death He saves us,
and lightens ev'ry load.

LO, HOW A ROSE E'ER BLOOMING

TRADITIONAL

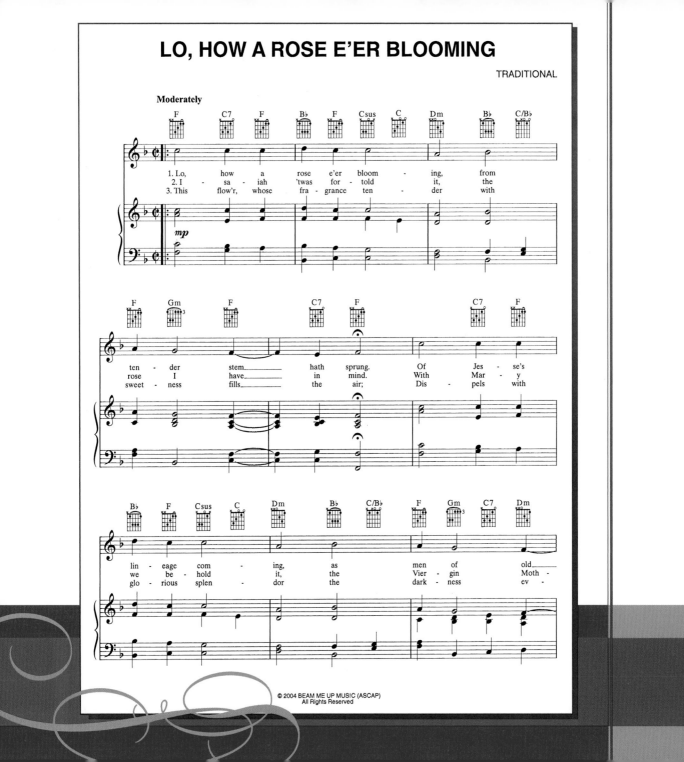

The First Nowell

Other title:
The First Noël
Words & Music:
Anonymous,
sixteenth-century
English folk song

The title of this beloved carol is often spelled "The First Noël," giving rise to the common misconception that the song is of French origin. But "The First Nowell" is the correct spelling. The word *noël* comes from the Latin word *natalis,* and is commonly thought of as a French translation for "Christmas carol." "Nowell" is an English word dating back as far as the fourteenth century, when Geoffrey Chaucer (1340–1400) used the term in his medieval masterpiece *The Canterbury Tales.* Most likely originating in the Cornwall region of southwest England in the sixteenth century, the words for this shepherd song were not published until 1823, and the music in 1833. The origin of the tune remains a mystery; it is the type of joyous Christmas song that would have been suppressed by the Puritans in the mid-seventeenth century. The refrain of the 1833 melody was revised by the 1870s, with the current smooth notes for the words "born is the King" replacing an uninspired passage. Over time, "The First Nowell" has become one of the finest of English carols.

There is a carol called "The First Noël" that reputedly comes from Cornwall as well, with lyrics quite similar to those of "The First Nowell." Nevertheless, the two are separate and distinct songs.

The first Nowell, the angels did say,
was to certain poor shepherds in fields as they lay;
In fields where they lay keeping their sheep,
on a cold winter's night that was so deep.
REFRAIN:
Nowell, nowell, nowell, nowell;
Born is the King of Israel.

They looked up and saw a star
shining in the East beyond them far;
And to the earth it gave great light,
and so it continued day and night.
REFRAIN

And by the light of that same star,
three wise men came from country far;
To seek for a king was their intent,
and to follow the star where ever it went.
REFRAIN

This star drew nigh to the northwest;
O'er Bethlehem it took its rest.
And there it did both stop and stay,
right o'er the place where Jesus lay.
REFRAIN

Then did they know assuredly
within that house the King did lie:
One entered in then for to see,
aAnd found the babe in poverty.
REFRAIN

Then entered in those wise men three,
full reverently upon their knee,
and offered there in His presence
their gold and myrrh and frankincense.
REFRAIN

Between an ox-stall and an ass
this child truly there born he was;
For want of clothing they did him lay
all in the manger, among the hay:
REFRAIN

Then let us all with one accord
sing praises to our heavenly Lord,
that hath made heaven and earth of naught,
and with his blood mankind hath bought:
REFRAIN

If we in our time shall do well,
we shall be free from death and hell;
For God hath prepared for us all
a resting place in general
REFRAIN

THE FIRST NOEL

Messiah

Chorus: Hallelujah

Words: Biblical texts selected by Charles Jennens (1700–1773), English poet and librettist
Music: George Frederic Handel (1685–1759), German-born English composer

Perhaps the most famous chorus ever composed, whose text comes mostly from the book of Revelation in the New Testament, the "Hallelujah Chorus" is a magnificent piece that clearly states Handel's unmistakable faith in his Lord God truly reigning over this world. Although the primary emphasis of the "Hallelujah Chorus" is on the later years of Christ's life, the oratorio is more universally sung and celebrated during the Christmas season. This is not a unique development—in the middle ages, the death and resurrection of Christ were often commemorated in mystery plays and carols during the Christmas season.

Hallelujah!
For the Lord God omnipotent reigneth.
The kingdom of this world is become
the kingdom of our Lord,
and of His Christ;
And He shall reign for ever and ever.
King of Kings, and Lord of Lords
Hallelujah!

HALLELUJAH CHORUS
Chorus from "The Messiah"

by
GEORGE FREDERICK HANDEL

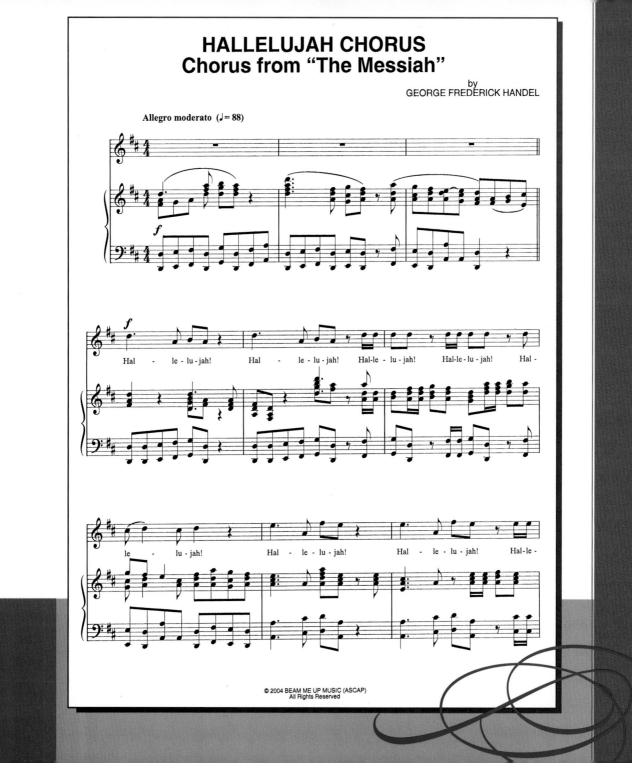

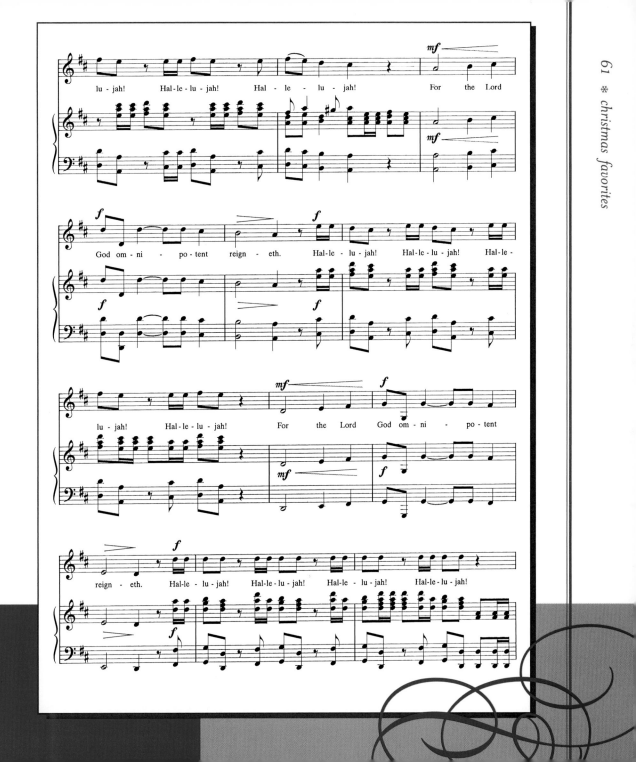

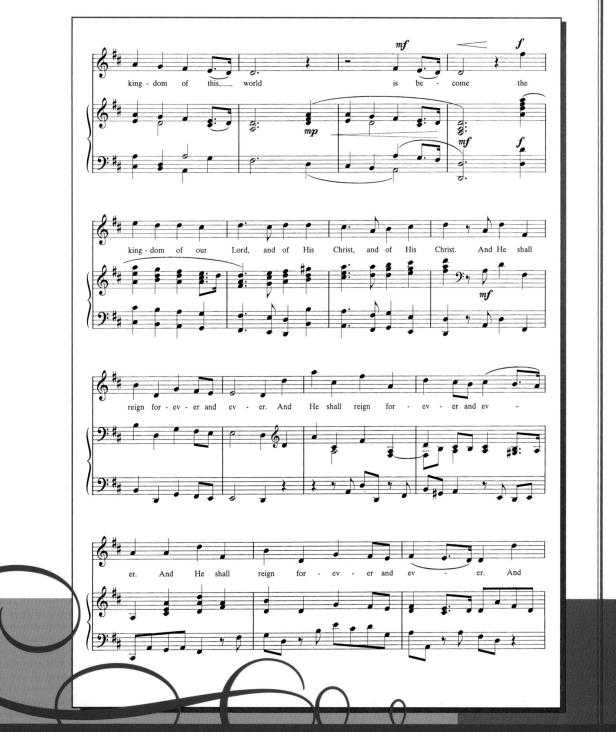

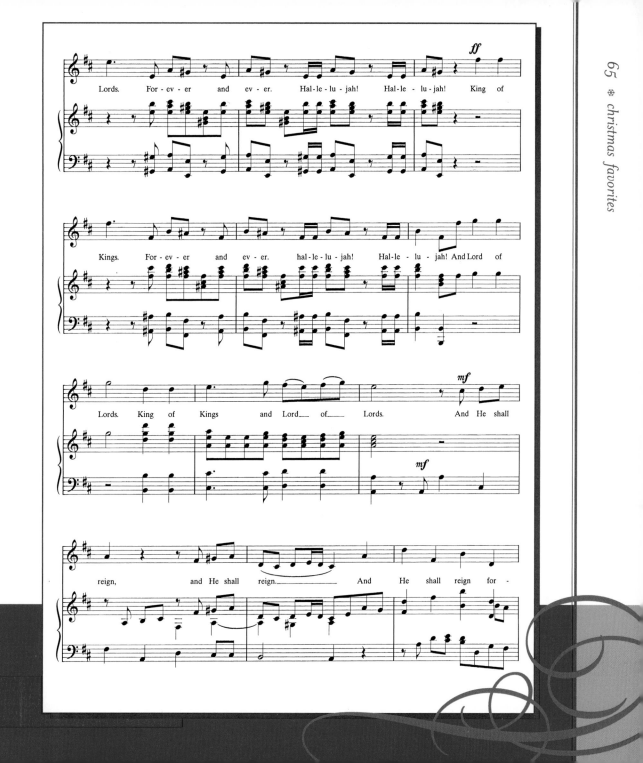

What Child Is This?

Words: William Chatterton Dix (1837–1898), English clergyman
Music: Anonymous, sixteenth century English folk song

The famous medieval tune of "Greensleeves" forms the basis of the lovely carol "What Child Is This?" One of the earliest references to the tune was in 1580 when it was mentioned several times in Shakespeare's comedy play *The Merry Wives of Windsor*. Strains of the music can also be heard in the 1728 satirical ballad opera *The Beggar's Opera*, by John Gay (1685–1732).

Religiously inspired, William Chatterton Dix wrote his lyrics around 1865 as a six-stanza poem titled "The Manger Throne." Later he took three of the poem's stanzas and adapted them to the popular sixteenth-century tune of "Greensleeves." In 1871, the text was published in Bramley & Stainer's *Christmas Carols, New and Old,* a highly popular compilation. The legacy of "What Child Is This?" has been sustained over the years by its unforgettable beauty.

What Child is this, who laid to rest,
on Mary's lap is sleeping?
Whom angels greet with anthems sweet
while shepherds watch are keeping?
This, this is Christ the King,
whom shepherds guard and angels Sing.
Haste, haste to bring Him laud,
the Babe, the Son of Mary.

Why lies He in such mean estate
where ox and ass are feeding?
Good Christians, fear for sinners here
the silent Word is pleading.
Nails, spear shall pierce Him through;
The cross He bore, for me, for you.
Hail, hail the Word made Flesh,
the Babe, the Son of Mary.

So bring Him incense, gold and myrrh;
Come, peasant king, to own Him.
The King of Kings salvation brings;
Let loving hearts enthrone Him.
Raise, raise the song on high,
the Virgin sings her lullaby.
Joy, joy for Christ is born,
the Babe, the Son of Mary.

WHAT CHILD IS THIS?

By WILLIAM C. DIX
Based on GREENSLEVES.
An Old English Air

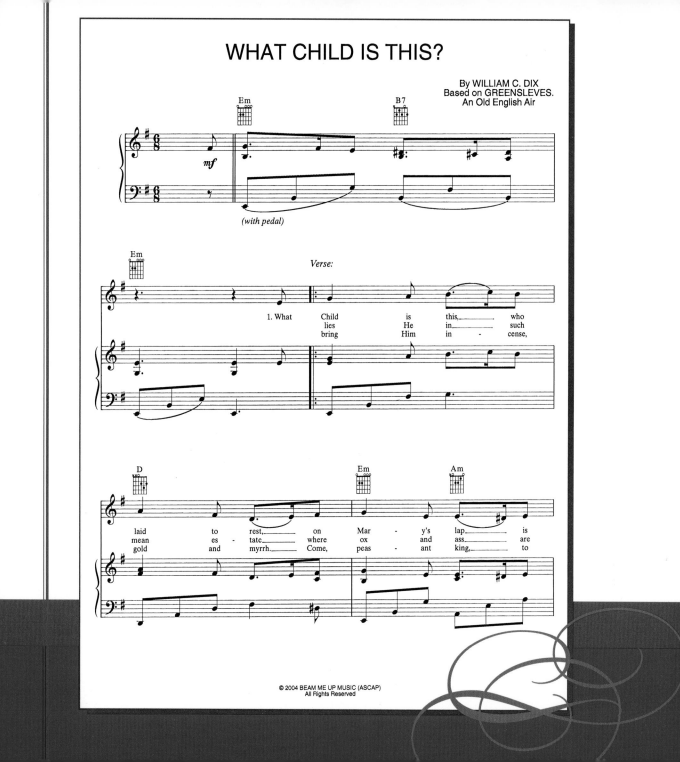

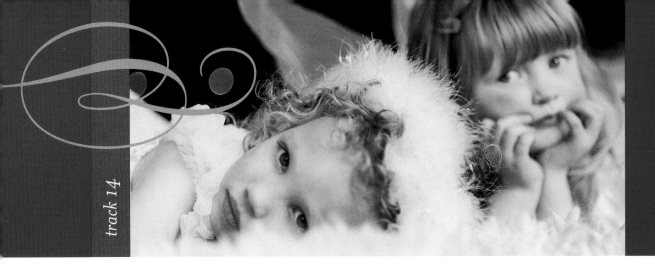

Hark! The Herald Angels Sing

Words: Charles Wesley (1707–1788), English author and poet
Music: Felix Mendelssohn (1809–1847), German composer

Hark! The Herald Angels Sing" was originally titled "Hymn for Christmas Day" when it was written by Charles Wesley as a poem in 1739. Wesley—one of eighteen children born of a modest family—along with his brother, John (1703–1791), was an important figure in the founding of Methodism. In addition, he published about 4,430 hymns and wrote thousands more preserved only in manuscript. His most famous collection was *Hymns for the Use of the People Called Methodists*.

The first line of the poem, "Hark, how all the welkin rings" ("welkin" in Old English means "heavens"), was changed fourteen years after its publication by George Whitefield (1714–1770), an Anglican clergyman (who also co-founded Dartmouth College in Hanover, New Hampshire). More lines of Wesley's poem were revised in later years. Charles Wesley himself brought changes to the original poem by expanding it from four to ten stanzas.

William Cummings (1831–1915), an organist at Waltham Abbey, adapted the melody by Felix Mendelssohn to Wesley's hymn because he felt the two went nicely together and first presented it on Christmas Day in 1855. His arrangement is generally used today. Mendelssohn, who objected to Cummings using his music, had been commissioned to compose the music for the 1840 Leipzig Gutenberg Festival commemorating the four hundredth anniversary of the invention of the printing press and the first book printed by Johann Gutenberg—a Latin translation of the Bible. Against this interesting backdrop, "Hark! The Herald Angels Sing" emerges as one of our more expressively joyful Christmas carols.

Hark! The herald angels sing,
"Glory to the newborn King!
Peace on earth and mercy mild,
God and sinners reconciled."
Joyful, all ye nations rise,
join the triumph of the skies;
With angelic host proclaim,
"Christ is born in Bethlehem!"
REFRAIN:
Hark, the herald angels sing,
"Glory to the newborn King!"

Christ by highest heav'n adored;
Christ the everlasting Lord!
Late in time behold Him come,
offspring of a Virgin's womb.
Veiled in flesh the Godhead see;
Hail the incarnate Deity.
Pleased as man with man to dwell,
Jesus, our Emmanuel!
REFRAIN

Hail the heav'n-born Prince of Peace!
Hail the Son of Righteousness!
Light and life to all He brings,
ris'n with healing in His wings.
Mild He lays His glory by.
Born that man no more may die.
Born to raise the sons of earth;
Born to give them second birth.
REFRAIN

Come Desire of Nations come,
fix in us Thy humble home;
Rise the woman's conquering seed,
bruise in us the serpent's head.
Now display Thy saving power,
ruin'd nature now restore.
Now in mystic union join
Thine to ours and ours to Thine.
REFRAIN

Adam's likeness, Lord, efface;
Stamp Thy image in its place.
Second Adam from above,
reinstate us in Thy love.
Let us Thee though lost regain,
then the Life, the Inner Man.
O! to all Thyself impart,
form'd in each believing heart.
REFRAIN

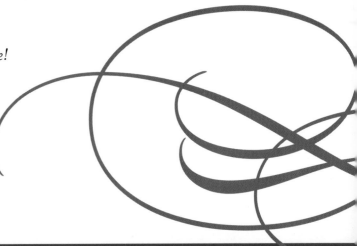

HARK! THE HERALD ANGELS SING

Words by
CHARLES WESLEY

Music by
FELIX MENDELSSOHN

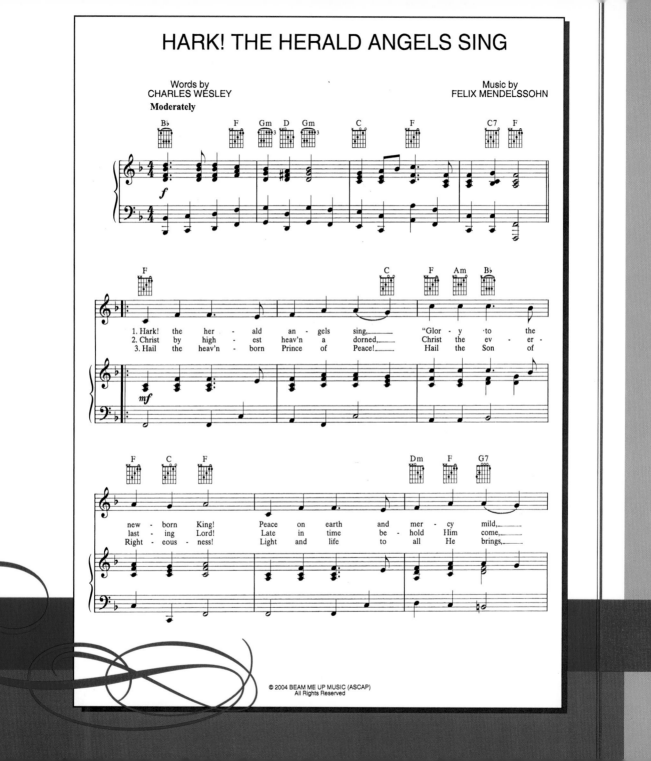

Silent Night

German Title: Stille Nacht
Words: Joseph Mohr
(1792–1848),
Austrian priest
Music: Franz Gruber
(1787–1863), Austrian
church organist

Perhaps the best-known Christmas carol of all time, having been translated into forty-four different languages, "Silent Night" has several interesting accounts of its creation. The most popular one, authenticated by Franz Gruber himself, claims that the song was written quickly by Gruber on Christmas Eve in 1818 with lyrics by the Rev. Joseph Mohr, of St. Nicholas Church of Obendorf, Austria, after the organ of their small village church had broken down. Needing music for the church service, these two improving souls, the legend holds, came up with a melody for two solo voices, a chorus, and a guitar. It became one of our most devotional carols.

Another account has a more sacred tone. The Rev. Mohr's inspiration came on the night a child was born in the house of a young woodsman of his parish. At the behest of the anxious father, the priest quickly plodded through the snow to bring words of good cheer and blessings for the young mother and the house. The Rev. Mohr, though weary from the trek through the heavy snow, was impressed by the pervasive and comforting silence of the starry night. Upon his arrival at the woodsman's humble abode, he was further moved when he gazed upon the small, rough-hewn cradle where the baby lay and the woodchopper tending to his wife at a nearby bed of pine logs.

The priest was transfixed by the scene and overcome by a feeling of radiance and holiness about the place. It struck him that the surroundings bore a strong resemblance to the birth of another child, the infant Jesus, as described eighteen hundred years earlier. After blessing the woodsman's home, the Rev. Mohr returned to his study and reflected on the scene he had just witnessed. While looking out across the snowy mountains and stars, he murmured to himself, "Stille nacht, heilige nacht." In this holy mood, he wrote the simple words of six stanzas that softly proclaimed the joy and peace of the first Christmas.

Several years after its initial Christmas eve performance, an organ repairman, hired to reconstruct the organ at St. Nicholas Church, apparently found a copy of the carol at the church and received permission to take it home with him. Soon after, traveling singing groups began to sing "Stille Nacht, Heilige Nacht" in different parts of Austria and ultimately in other regions of the world, spreading the carol's popularity. The song would become exceptionally popular in the United States after World War I, when returning war veterans remembered hearing it sung by German soldiers during Christmas truces.

The carol was probably first published between 1838 and 1840, in a collection of "four genuine Tyrolean songs." One English translation reduced it to three stanzas and a widely accepted version was completed in 1863 by the Rev. John Freeman Young (1820–1885), who later served as the Episcopal bishop of Florida in 1867.

The wonderful result of these developments was a simple, loving, tender song, resonating even today with the true meaning of Christmas. Is it any surprise, then, that "Silent Night" now ranks as the most-recorded carol in history?

Silent night, holy night,
all is calm, all is bright;
Round yon virgin mother and Child,
holy Infant so tender and mild,
sleep in heavenly peace,
sleep in heavenly peace.

Silent night, holy night,
shepherds quake at the sight;
Glories stream from heaven afar,
heavenly hosts sing Alleluia:
Christ, the Savior, is born!
Christ, the Savior, is born!

Silent night, holy night,
Son of God, Love's pure light;
Radiance beams from Thy holy face,
with the dawn of redeeming grace,
Jesus, Lord, at Thy birth.
Jesus, Lord, at Thy birth.

SILENT NIGHT

Words and Music by
JOSEPH MOHR and
FRANZ GRUBER

O Tannenbaum

English Title: O Christmas Tree
Words: Anonymous, sixteenth-
or seventeenth-century German folk
song for first verse; Ernest Gebhard
Anschutz (1800–1861), German
teacher, for other verses
Music: Anonymous, sixteenth- or
seventeenth-century German folk song

O Tannenbaum," perhaps the best-known carol from Germany, specifically refers to the Christmas tree, a much-celebrated symbol in tradition and song in Germany since the fifteenth or sixteenth century. Representing loyalty and fresh life, which was especially appreciated during winter's darkest days, the tradition of a Christmas tree dates back to the days of the Roman Empire when the evergreen was used in a decorative fashion during the period of the winter solstice in late December and early January.

Germans also used evergreens for pagan rituals celebrated at other times of the year. This is understandable, because the symbol of the evergreen was well rooted in the old religions of central Europe before they were totally eradicated by the early Christian Church. The earliest printed reference to decorating Christmas trees was a 1561 Alsatian ordinance that dictated how large an evergreen bush must be before it could be cut down.

Over the years the custom spread to the United States and Canada and became a firmly established tradition. Several legends have sprung from the tree trimming practice, including one that relates how all the trees of the world bore their best fruit on the night the Christ Child was born.

The original "O Tannenbaum" is believed to have had only one verse, the text for which appeared in an 1820 publication. Two other verses were added by Ernest Gebhard Anschutz in 1824 for his school children to sing, as Christmas trees had become common in his town of Leipzig. The melody belonged to an old Latin song that had been sung by German students for many generations prior to Anschutz's use of it.

The music has also been adopted for a number of different texts, including the song "Maryland, My Maryland." George K. Evans (b.1917), co-author of the well-researched 1963 text, *The International Book of Christmas Carols,* provides the English translation.

O Christmas tree, O Christmas tree,
you stand in verdant beauty!
O Christmas tree, O Christmas tree
you stand in verdant beauty!
Your boughs are green in summer's glow,
and do not fade in winter's snow.
O Christmas tree, O Christmas tree,
you stand in verdant beauty.

O Christmas tree, O Christmas tree,
how richly God has decked thee!
O Christmas tree, O Christmas tree,
how richly God has decked thee!
Thou bidst us true and faithful be,
and trust in God unchangingly.
O Christmas tree, O Christmas tree
how richly God has decked thee.

O Tannenbaum, O Tannenbaum,
wie treu sind deine Bläter.
O Tannenbaum, O Tannenbaum,
wie treu sind deine Bläter.
Du grünstnicht nur zur sommerzeit,
nein auch im winter wenn es schneit.
O Tannenbaum, O Tannenbaum,
wie treu sind deine Bläter.

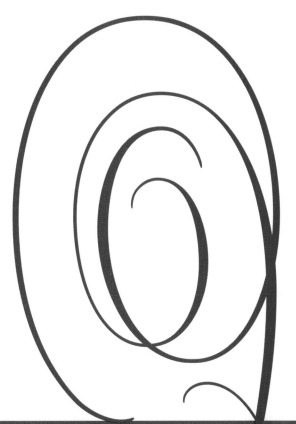

O CHRISTMAS TREE
(O Tannenbaum)

OLD GERMAN CAROL

Sleigh Ride

Words: Mitchell Parish
(1900–1993),
American songwriter
Music: Leroy Anderson
(1908–1975),
American composer

In 1950 Mitchell Parish added words to what was originally an instrumental piece by Leroy Anderson. Anderson composed the brilliant music in 1948, perhaps gaining inspiration by listening to Mozart's work of the same title. Both Parish and Anderson were noted for other popular works. Parish was responsible for the lyrics of the wistful and beautiful "Stardust," "Moonlight Serenade," and "Stairway to the Stars." Anderson, who also served as an arranger for the Boston Pops Orchestra, composed an interesting variety of unusual but well-crafted works, including "The Syncopated Clock," "Fiddle Faddle," "Bugler's Holiday," "The Typewriter," "Serenata," and "Blue Tango."

The instrumental "Sleigh Ride" is a light-hearted classic incorporating bells, horse whinnies, and whip cracking—sound effects that evoke the picturesque image of sleigh riding through the snowy countryside. The imagery of wintry holiday scenes was exquisitely captured by the popular lithographs of Currier & Ives in the mid-to-late nineteenth century, as referred to in the lyrics.

Just hear those sleigh bells jingling, ring ting tingling too;
Come on, it's lovely weather for a sleigh ride together with you.
Outside, the snow is falling and friends are calling "Yoo-hoo";
Come on, it's lovely weather for a sleigh ride together with you.

Giddy-yap, giddy-yap, giddy-yap, let's go;
Let's look at the show.
We're riding in a wonderland of snow.
Giddy-yap, giddy-yap, giddy-yap it's grand,
just holding your hand;
We're gliding along with a song of a wintery fairyland.

Our cheeks are nice and rosy, and comfy cozy are we;
We're snuggled up together like two birds of a feather would be.
Let's take that road before us and sing a chorus or two;
Come on, it's lovely weather for a sleigh ride together with you.

There's a birthday party at the home of Farmer Gray;
It'll be a perfect ending of a perfect day.
We'll be singing the songs we love to sing without a single stop,
at the fireplace while we watch the chestnuts pop, pop, pop, pop.

There's a happy feeling nothing in the world can buy,
when they pass around the coffee and the pumpkin pie.
It'll nearly be like a picture print by Currier and Ives.
These wonderful things are the things we remember all thru' our lives.

Just hear those sleigh bells jingling, ring ting tingling too;
Come on, it's lovely weather for a sleigh ride together with you.
Outside, the snow is falling and friends are calling "Yoo-hoo";
Come on, it's lovely weather for a sleigh ride together with you.

Giddy-yap, giddy-yap, giddy-yap, let's go;
Let's look at the show.
We're riding in a wonderland of snow.
Giddy-yap, giddy-yap, giddy-yap it's grand,
just holding your hand;
We're gliding along with a song of a wintery fairyland.

Our cheeks are nice and rosy and comfy cozy are we;
We're snuggled up together like two birds of a feather would be.
Let's take the road before us and sing a chorus or two;
Come on, it's lovely weather for a sleigh ride together with you.

SLEIGH RIDE

Words by
MITCHELL PARISH

Music by
LEROY ANDERSON